ANGEL SOULZ   JAY BOGICEVIC

SOUL OF LIGHT

POETRY & SONG LYRICS

deeply silent

AF208890

ANGEL SOULZ   JAY BOGICEVIC

SOUL OF LIGHT

POETRY & SONG LYRICS

deeply silent

Bibliografische Information der Deutschen Nationalbibliothek:
Die Deutsche Nationalbibliothek verzeichnet diese Publikation in der
Deutschen Nationalbibliografie; detaillierte bibliografische Daten sind im
Internet über http://dnb.dnb.de abrufbar.

Herstellung und Verlag: BoD – Books on Demand, Norderstedt

ISBN: 978-3-7568-6990-9

This is more than just a book,
it's readable art.

Dies ist mehr als nur ein Buch,
es ist lesbare Kunst.

03:33 AM

I'M LOSING MY MIND
IN A WORLD SO COLD
LIKE THERE IS NO SOUL
LIKE MINE TO FIND

NO SOUL WHO LOVES
LIKE I DO

ANGEL SOULZ   JAY BOGICEVIC

I used to overthink a lot
how other people see me.
I think what's most important
is... how I see myself.

Love yourself first.

Ich habe zu viel darüber nachgedacht,
wie andere Menschen mich sehen.
Ich denke am wichtigsten ist es,
wie ich mich selbst sehe.

Liebe dich selbst zuerst.

Jay Bogicevic

Every morning of our lives brings
a new beginning.
What we do and say on each new day
reveals
who we are and who we want to be.

Jeder Morgen in unserem Leben
ist ein neuer Anfang.
Was wir an jedem neuen Tag tun und sagen,
deckt auf,
wer wir sind und wer wir sein wollen.

Jay Bogicevic

03:03 AM

SOMETIMES
THE UNIVERSE
TALKS BACK
BUT PEOPLE
DON'T LISTEN.

Angel Soulz

Sometimes I feel so lonely that only
the moon and the stars
can see my pain.

Manchmal fühle ich mich so einsam,
dass nur der Mond und die Sterne
meinen Schmerz sehen können.

Jay Bogicevic

05:03 AM

EVERY NIGHT BEFORE
I GO TO SLEEP
I PRAY TO GOD FOR YOU
TO GIVE YOU WHAT YOU NEED
EVEN IF IT'S NOT

ME

Angel Soul

MY TEARS FALL LIKE WATER

SO THAT I CAN GROW
SO THAT I CAN GROW

TO BE SOMEBODY
YOU'VE NEVER
SEEN BEFORE

Angel Soul

Never forget...

Vergiss nie...

Some nights can be beautiful
because the whole world
seems to be
silent.

Manche Nächte können wunderschön sein,
da die ganze Welt zu schweigen scheint.

...one voice becomes powerful.

...eine Stimme wird mächtig.

Jay Bogicevic

You are never alone,
your **higher self** is always with you.

Du bist nie allein,
dein **höheres Selbst** ist immer bei dir.

Jay Bogicevic

Listen…

Hör zu…

I SEE THE STARS FALLING
DOWN FROM HEAVEN
SUMMER NIGHTS SO COLD
IT FEELS LIKE WINTER
SUMMER NIGHTS
SUMMER NIGHTS
I TELL MYSELF THAT
I DON'T NEED YOU
I DON'T NEED YOU
I GOTTA FIND PEACE OF MIND

Angel Sulz

I CAN HEAR THE ANGELS
SCREAMING YOUR NAME
SO LOUD
THEY CAN'T FLY
WITH BROKEN WINGS

Angel Soulz

Speak less,
observe more.

    Sprich weniger,
    beobachte mehr.

       Jay Bogicevic

If you really look closely,
you'll see a pattern – in every
person's behavior.

Wenn du wirklich genau hinschaust,
wirst du ein Muster erkennen – in jedem
Verhalten des Menschen.

Jay Bogicevic

03:13 AM

You SWEAR You KNOW ME
BUT You DON'T KNOW
YOURSELF BABY

Angel Soulz

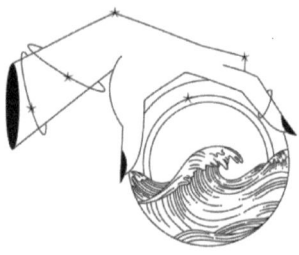

You are invulnerable,
when you have no expectations.

Du bist unverletzlich,
wenn du keine Erwartungen hast.

Jay Bogicevic

BABY YOU PRAY TO GOD
TO MAKE YOU ~~FEEL~~
ALIVE AGAIN
BUT YOU DON'T SEE
DON'T SEE
DON'T SEE
WHO I AM
WHO I AM BABY

Angel Soulz

Empty minds are like snakes,
they just wanna bite
you – silently.

Leere Köpfe sind wie Schlangen,
sie möchten dich nur beissen – schweigend.

Jay Bogicevic

I love how predictable people are.
You are readable, like a magazine.

Ich liebe es, wie berechenbar die Menschen sind.
Du bist lesbar, wie eine Zeitschrift.

Jay Bogicevic

I MATCH YOUR ENERGY
AND YOU GET UPSET
YOU ARE CRAZY LIKE THE
MAINSTREAM
HARD TO BELIEVE
IT'S LIKE A MATRIX
AND YOU CREATE IT
I SEE PATTERNS IN YOUR ACTION
BABY YOU ARE A REFLECTION
A MINDSET IS EVERYTHING
I READ YOU LIKE A MAGAZINE
NOW YOU'RE MAD AT ME
FOR BEING REAL
EGO BIGGER THAN IT SEEMS
PRIDE IS THE DEVIL
BUT I GUESS WE ARE
NOT ON THE SAME
LEVEL

Angel Soul

It's impossible to forget you
or even think of letting you go,
because the entire universe conspired
to help me find you.

Es ist unmöglich, dich zu vergessen
oder auch nur daran zu denken, dich loszulassen,
denn das ganze Universum hat sich verschworen,
um mir zu helfen, dich zu finden.

Jay Bogicevic

I often dance alone in my bedroom and use my
imagination to go to a party – far away from home.
You look at me at the same time as I look at you,
while my favorite song is playing in the background.
You smile – I smile.

Ich tanze oft allein in meinem Schlafzimmer und
nutze meine Vorstellungskraft, um auf eine Party
zu gehen – weit weg von zu Hause. Du siehst mich an,
zur gleichen Zeit, als ich dich ansehe, während mein
Lieblingssong im Hintergrund spielt.
Du lächelst – ich lächle.

Jay Bogicevic

I PRAY THAT YOU FEEL ALIVE
OH BABY HAPPINESS
IT COMES IN SO MANY WAYS
IT'S LIKE
WHEN I SEE YOU SMILE :)

Angel Soul

BABY YOU WANNA BE SOMEBODY
YOU WANNA BE SOMEBODY
SO SO BAD
AND I JUST WANNA SAY
I'M SO PROUD OF YOU
YOU DO THE THINGS
THAT I CAN'T DO

I NEVER SEE YOU
BUT THE MOVES YOU DO
THE SPIRIT IS DIFFERENT
IT AIN'T FREE
LOVERS AND FRIENDS
IS WHAT WE COULD BE
BUT YOU AIN'T FAIR
IT'S ALL IN MY HEAD

Angel Soulz

03:27 AM

SHE SAID
I SHOULD KEEP MY FEELINGS
TO MYSELF
I LET THAT SH*T GO BABY
I LET THAT SH*T GO

Angel Soul

I like listening to everyone,
but mostly I love to listen to my inner voice.

Ich mag es allen zuzuhören,
aber am liebsten höre ich meiner
inneren Stimme zu.

Jay Bogicevic

03:03 AM

I'M TIRED OF THIS NEWS
I'M TIRED OF THESE
FAKE SPIRITUAL PEOPLE
I'M TALKING ABOUT
THEY KNOW EVERTHING
BUT DON'T SEE
THE BIGGER PICTURE

Angel Soul

I JUST DON'T KNOW WHAT TO SAY
I JUST DON'T KNOW WHAT TO ~~FEEL~~
I KNOW I'M LOSING MY MIND
CAUSE YOU KNOW WHY
BABY I'M LOSING MY MIND
I'M LOSING MY MIND EVERYDAY
WHEN I WATCH THE NEWS
AND I GO CRAZY LIKE

Angel Soul

Just being **ME** is the key.

Einfach **ICH** zu sein ist der Schlüssel.

Jay Bogicevic

FOR FREEDOM AND PEACE OF MIND
THE PEOPLE ARE RISING
THE STREETS ARE FULL
THE LIGHT IS ON
BABY WHAT YOU GONNA DO

I'M NOT OBSESSED WITH YOU
I'M OBSESSED WITH PROTECTING YOU
DON'T YOU SEE IT COMING
THEY WANNA TAKE CONTROL
OVER ME AND YOU
NAH DEVIL NOT TODAY
NEVA EVA

Angel Soul

I PRAY FOR FREEDOM
OH I PRAY FOR FREEDOM
GOD YOU KNOW
THE WORLD IS SO SO BLIND
SO BLIND
THEY FIGHT OVER LITTLE THINGS
LIKE IT MATTERS
THEY DON'T SEE THE BIGGER PICTURE
OH GOD FORGIVE US

IT'S SO SAD TO SEE THE WORLD
LIKE THIS
THEY TURN ANGELS INTO DEVILS
OH THEY DO
OH GOD YOU KNOW
THIS WORLD IS SO UNREAL
SO UNREAL
MAKE IT GO AWAY
ALL MY PAIN
OH YOU KNOW THAT I FEEL
MORE THAN ANYBODY ELSE
OH YOU SEE IT IN ME
OH I'M READY TO SHOW THE WORLD
WHO I CAN BE

Angel Soul

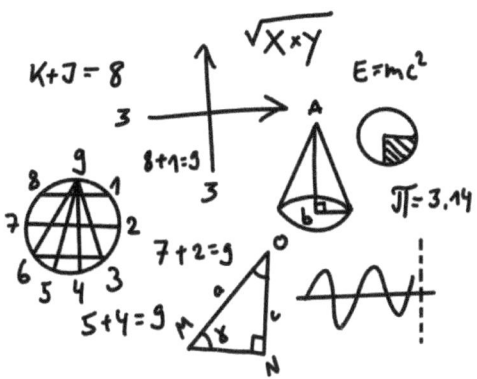

No one can be you.
Your existence is bigger than any algorithm.

Niemand kann du sein.
Deine Existenz ist grösser als jeder Algorithmus.

Jay Bogicevic

She is like a drug.
My mind screamed: **Go to rehab!**
My heart said peacefully: **Don't.**
It was as if my higher self was fighting a battle
with the idiot inside me.

Sie ist wie eine Droge.
Mein Verstand schrie: **Mach einen Entzug!**
Mein Herz sagte friedlich: **Tu es nicht.**
Es war, als ob mein höheres Selbst einen Kampf
austragen würde mit dem Idioten in mir.

Jay Bogicevic

I'M TIRED OF THE SAME OLD SONGS
You LIKE TO PRESS PLAY IN MY MIND
YOU REPEAT YOURSELF ALL THE TIME
YOU THINK YOU KNOW ME WELL
BUT LET ME TELL
IT AIN'T THAT WAY BABY

YOU WANT TO SEE ME LOSE
I WANT TO SEE YOU WIN
WE DIFFERENT BABY
WE - WE AIN'T THE SAME

YOU MAKE FUN OF ME
I THINK HOW STUPID I CAN BE
YOU MADE ME BELIEVE
FAIRY TALES AND MAGIC EXIST

Angel Soul

YOU LOVE TO PLAY WITH HEARTS – I SEE
YOU LIKE TO BREAK THEM SO EASILY
YOU DON'T GIVE A F**K
WHAT YOU DID TO ME
TAKE A LOOK IN THE MIRROR
DO YOU STILL KNOW WHO YOU ARE

Angel Soul

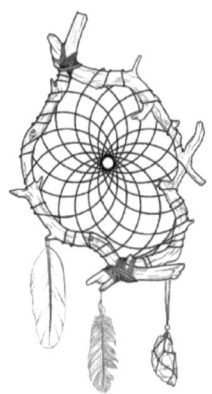

My dreams feel like days I get to spend with you.
So my heart starts playing games with my mind.
The more I try to distance myself from you in
the real world, the longer the days in my dreams
with you become.

Meine Träume fühlen sich wie Tage an, die ich mit dir
verbringen darf. So beginnt mein Herz, mit meinem
Verstand Spiele zu spielen. Je mehr ich versuche,
mich in der realen Welt von dir zu distanzieren,
desto länger werden die Tage in meinen Träumen
mit dir.

Jay Bogicevic

SOMETIMES I'M COLD
AND I DON'T THINK
SAYING SH*T I DON'T MEAN
I FEEL LIKE THAT'S NOT ME
BUT TELL ME WHO IT IS

WHO MADE ME LIKE THIS
YOU DON'T KNOW
IT'S THE WORLD AND THE PAIN I FEEL
IT'S THE PAST AND THE PEOPLE
PLAYING GAMES WITH ME

NOW I SEE IT CRISTAL CLEAR
I SEE THE FUTURE VERSION OF ME
IT'S LIKE A F**KING SONG
ON REPEAT
I KNOW WHO I NEED TO BE
YOU DON'T SEE
WHAT GOD SEES IN ME

Angel Soul

I don't know where this is going or
how the chapter will end, but I know
one thing for sure: This magic that stands
between us, we will not experience a second time
on this earth. We both know...

Ich weiss nicht, wohin das führt oder
wie das Kapitel enden wird, aber eins weiss ich
mit Sicherheit: Diese Magie, die zwischen uns steht,
werden wir kein zweites Mal auf dieser Erde erleben.
Das wissen wir beide...

Jay Bogicevic

A funny tarot card reader told me to let go,
but you know, I don't like people telling me
what to do.

Ein lustiger Tarotkartenleser sagte mir,
ich solle loslassen, aber du weisst ja,
dass ich es nicht mag, wenn mir Menschen sagen,
was ich tun soll.

Jay Bogicevic

03:33 AM

BABY I'M LOSING MY MIND
IN A WORLD SO COLD
LIKE THERE IS NO SOUL
LIKE MINE TO FIND
NO SOUL WHO LOVES LIKE I DO
NO FREEDOM IN MY MIND

THE WORLD GETS COLDER
DAY BY DAY
EVERYONE SEES IT
NO ONE BELIEVES IT
LOOK AT THIS SH*T
WE'RE CALLING LOVE THESE DAYS

Angel Soul

THE PICTURE UNCLEAR
HOW YOU SEE ME
YOU MIGHT THINK I'M CRAZY
BUT IT'S ALL LOVE
I HOPE YOU SEE IT

Angel Soulz

My darling,
the bare minimum is not effort,
like attention is not love.

Mein Schatz,
das blosse Minimum ist keine Anstrengung,
so wie Aufmerksamkeit keine Liebe ist.

Jay Bogicevic

To live a life we deserve,
we need to understand – what love really is.

Um ein Leben zu leben, das wir verdienen,
müssen wir verstehen – was Liebe wirklich ist.

Jay Bogicevic

I am very likely
your best chapter - write a good ending.

Ich bin sehr wahrscheinlich
dein bestes Kapitel - schreib ein gutes Ende.

Jay Bogicevic

ANGEL SOULZ   JAY BOGICEVIC

SOUL OF LIGHT

POETRY & SONG LYRICS

introvertly

I thought I saw a light in you
but it seems like
I was just – delusional.

Ich dachte ich habe ein Licht
in dir gesehen,
aber wie es scheint,
hatte ich nur – Wahnvorstellungen.

Jay Bogicevic